THE CHAMPION PIG

THE CHAMPION PIG

Great Moments in Everyday Life
by Barbara P. Norfleet

David R. Godine ☆ Publisher ☆ Boston

DAVID R. GODINE · PUBLISHER
306 Dartmouth Street
Boston, Massachusetts 02116

ISBN: 0-87923-269-2 (hc); 0-87923-270-6 (sc)
LCC NO: 78-73656

The Champion Pig was designed by Katy Homans,
typeset by Michael & Winifred Bixler, and
printed by The Meriden Gravure Company.

Frontispiece: Harry Annas Studio ★ *Lockhart, Texas, 1948*

Printed in the United States of America

★ ACKNOWLEDGMENTS

RESEARCH FOR THIS BOOK and the exhibition that accompanies it began more than three years ago when I received a grant from the National Endowment for the Humanities to set up an archive on the social history of America as recorded by studio photographers. The pictures were collected from negative files in studios throughout America. It was exciting to see how local professional photographers captured this country's diversity and complexity in carrying out their daily work.

The photographs included in *The Champion Pig* were printed from negatives found in the files of sixteen of these studios. I would like to express my deepest thanks to the following photographers for giving me access to their files:

Harry Annas   *Lockhart, Texas*
Bradford Bachrach   *East Coast*
Orrion Barger   *Chamberlain, South Dakota*
Samuel Cooper   *Brookline, Massachusetts*
John Deusing   *West Allis, Wisconsin*
George Durette   *Manchester, New Hampshire*
Paul Gittings   *Houston and Dallas, Texas*
W. E. A. Moore (Hamblin Studio)   *Suffolk, Virginia*
Ina Porter (O. B. Porter Studio)   *Houlton, Maine*
Eugenie Ragan (C. Bennette Moore Studio)   *New Orleans, Louisiana*
Jack Rodden   *Roswell, New Mexico*
Martin Schweig   *St. Louis, Missouri*
Joe Steinmetz   *Sarasota, Florida*
Francis Sullivan   *Derry, New Hampshire*
Delmar Watson   *Hollywood, California*
Terry Wood   *Tupelo, Mississippi*

The generous cooperation of these talented photographers made this book possible.

For their individual help and support I thank the following individuals: Bobbi Carrey and Adrienne Linden, who assisted me in the early period of researching studio negative files; Arthur Heitzman, at the Gittings Studio, and Michael Milakovich, at the Deusing Studio, who helped me as I collected from their studios; Chris Burnett, who untiringly made prints from the negatives, copied nitrate negatives, and helped the project along in many other ways; Lise Newcomer, Ted Cartselos, Chris Gerolmo, and Joe Bartschera, who made contacts of the large number of negatives; and Hilary Horton, who edited my manuscript. I thank Bradford Bachrach, Brian Berglund, Bobbi Carrey, Ted Cartselos, Timothy Cohn, Patsy Degener, William Ewing, Wendy Moonan, Sayre Sheldon, and Chris Tilghman for sharing their ideas with me. For encouragement and counsel I would especially like to thank John Szarkowski.

I want to acknowledge my debt to David Riesman, whose brilliant scholarship and observations on America influenced me enormously during the many years I taught with him at Harvard University.

I express my thanks to the Carpenter Center for the Visual Arts at Harvard University for its continuing support of photography and of The Photography Archive. I am also grateful to the Center's staff—Heather Ebey, Marjorie Kane, Roberta Murphy, and Cynthia von Thuna—for their administrative and secretarial assistance.

With a generous grant, the National Endowment of the Arts has encouraged the publication of this book and the exhibition of the larger collection of photographs that accompanies it. The National Endowment for the Humanities has also provided substantial aid, enabling me to research the negative files of selected professional photographers.

—B. P. N.

Paul Gittings Studio ★ *Dallas, Texas, c. 1930's*

★ INTRODUCTION

WHEN I WAS A CHILD I lived in a small resort town in southern New Jersey that was hit hard by the Depression. Families contracted: the households of my friends included parents and children, grandparents, an uncle, an aunt, and a cousin or two. My family moved in with my French grandfather because he had a job as a chef, and with it came a tiny house for all of us to live in.

The town had a few rich people and some middle-class people such as my grandfather, and many who had been poor or else became so because of the Depression. I learned very early to tell these groups apart by their possessions, their smells, and how they carried themselves; but the outstanding differences were in the expressions on their faces.

The faces of the poor showed vulnerability, confusion, distrust, and fear; the faces of the rich showed immunity to the caprices of life, the assurance of those who control their fate. My grandfather and others like him with steady jobs displayed a clear-eyed, if guarded, confidence that things would work out all right as long as they worked hard enough and maintained good living habits.

The people in this collection of photographs are sheltered in the middle and upper classes. They exhibit the same self-confidence as the safely employed and the rich of my childhood. These are people who believed they controlled their lives; they seem immune to events, and, at the moment their pictures were taken, they had no doubts or fears about what the camera would find.

These photographs were made by studio photographers mostly working outside the studio; the people in the pictures were, with a few exceptions, the photographer's clients. Hired for moments of significance—of triumph—by those who could afford his service, the studio photographer makes portraits and records social rituals in middle- and upper-class America.

Documentary photography has tended to portray a different America. The documentary photographer is not invited to pierce the veil of privacy of those who have power and security; he or she usually finds it easier and more rewarding to concentrate on poor people, recent immigrants, exploited children, drug users, strippers, or freaks. This work might be supported by the government, an educational institution, or a publisher, or the photographer might finance his picture taking with some unrelated job. He is not paid by his subjects and his subjects seldom see his results. He often has a point of view—his effort to portray the downtrodden sometimes exalts them—but he aspires to make truthful, unembellished images of directly observed fact. The motive of the documentary photographer may be the desire to bring about reform: if he provides accurate evidence of slums, child labor, prejudice, and despair, social wrongs might be corrected. In compiling convincing records of what he sees, the gifted documentary photographer sometimes produces a work of art. His audience is newspaper or magazine readers, social historians, and art lovers.

In contrast, the studio photographer creates formal portraits composed under artificial lights with fixed backgrounds and props. The pictures are printed from negatives retouched to display a person who is younger, more beautiful—more perfect—than the subject. The studio photographer must respond to the character, aspirations, and attitudes of his customer if he is going to please him. Essential to this task is a knowledge of the iconography, fantasies, and myths of the culture he is visually preserving. He must photograph exactly what his customer takes seriously.

Less well known is the work of the studio photographer

that is done outside the studio. Using a smaller, hand-held camera, he records for his clients, who are in the mainstream of American life, those moments and rituals of great personal importance — weddings, graduations, birthdays, a first haircut. In this the photographer is bridging the work of the studio and the street: his subjects are paying him and posing, but the approach is much less structured than inside the studio — the occasions recorded, the settings, the clothing of the subjects are much more varied, offering the photographer a broader choice in how he captures what he sees. As in documentary photographs, the prints are made from sharp, unretouched negatives, and they depict, in exquisite detail, telling aspects of American life.

In trying to look their best, the paying subjects portrayed outside the formalized studio play a role in accentuating, rather than retouching, reality. The man on page 2 exudes a confidence conferred by money and position. He knows that he is presenting that confidence to the camera. He and the photographer have chosen a posture and setting that emphasize this message, at the same time giving us a glimpse into the world of power in America. The photographer has both pleased the customer and produced a social document.

The pictures in this book start with the end of the nineteen-twenties, cover the Depression years, and progress through an increasingly comfortable period of prosperity for America's middle class, stopping before the upheavals of the late sixties. The Crash, bread lines, Hitler, and the atomic bomb do not appear in these photographs. The pictures are of events people chose to remember. And yet, selective though they are, these photographs reveal a great deal. In them we see the vast diversity of middle-class Americans: people whose differences derive from income, occupation, religion, sex, region, and ethnicity. The couple on page 59 and the men on page 87 wanted to be portrayed in relation to their horses, but the differences between the results are more striking than the

similarities. The boy and girl on pages 24 and 25 are about the same age, both are middle-class, and both chose studio photographs, and yet they have two very distinct notions as to what should be recorded.

Finding these pictures was a little like searching for a hidden haystack and then looking for the needle. Bradford Bachrach, now retired from the venerable photographic firm, provided me with the names of many old photographers whose work he admired. Other photographers were located by tracking down the children and grandchildren of those who were listed in *Outstanding Professional Photographers of America*, published in 1940; if these descendants were also photographers, the chances were good that the negatives made by their parents and grandparents had not been scattered or destroyed. Several photographers whose work I collected suggested other studios I should look at. The more talented professionals knew each other and wanted to help.

I especially liked to locate photographers in the smaller towns and cities of America, for the photographer in such communities plays a special role. Often, in addition to his studio work, he takes pictures for newspapers or does crime photography for the police. He is a recognized and important member of the community; he records its life, and his work spans generations. The day I phoned Orrion Barger in Chamberlain, South Dakota, to see if he could tell me how to find Betty (page 30), a subject photographed in 1948, Betty's daughter came into his studio to have her senior high-school picture taken. He now records the weddings of children whose parents he photographed when they were married, and, when they are born, the grandchildren will also be photographed. Orrion Barger can even persuade divorced parents to stand together to complete a wedding album.

When I came upon a professional photographer who does or did interesting work, the search became exciting, but also tiring. It takes a number of long days to go through negative files (the prints went to the clients), for old studios frequently have over a million negatives. There is a heavy concentration on marriage, death, baptism, graduation, family reunions, golden anniversaries, and retirement parties, and such important events as getting a bike, receiving a prize, or going to a prom. The good studio photographer combines content with art; he has many fine pictures on each of these subjects.

My various methods of discovering photographers failed to locate any within this time framework who belonged to a minority group. While the work of the photographers in this collection does include a few portraits of minority-group members, they were by and large represented only as they contributed to white middle-class American life.

I have ordered these photographs chronologically by the ages of the people portrayed. My intention is simply to explore the rich complexity of American life; I do not mean to imply that mankind is one loving family that shares basic yearnings.

It would be a mistake to think that these pictures can provide any definitive truths about America. Photographs are better at raising questions than at answering them; they can reveal what you do not understand, and also what you take for granted. It is possible to analyze a photograph as a work of art or for its information on material culture because all the information you need is in the photograph, but to interpret the picture's meaning requires information outside the photograph. Like the historian, who edits his raw material, the photographer chooses his subject, frames it to include and exclude, and at the moment he sees fit, clicks his shutter. The result of this interaction between *a person with a camera* and *a subject* at a particular *time and place* is then seen by *the viewer*, who also edits the photograph as he filters it—unconsciously—through his frame of reference. Most of us, of course, do not think about what we are bringing to a photograph when we look at it, but rather respond to it as a simple copy of nature. I have chosen four photographs that demonstrate, each in its own way, how difficult it is to unriddle what we see.

Joe Steinmetz Studio ⋆ *Sarasota, Florida, 1957*

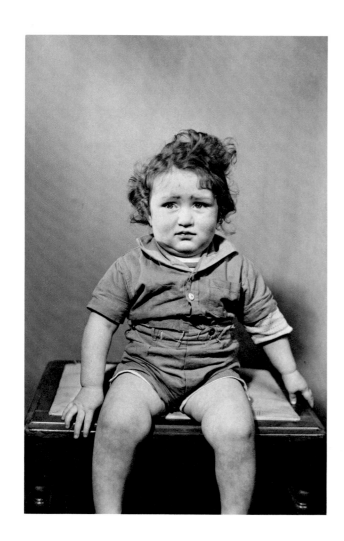
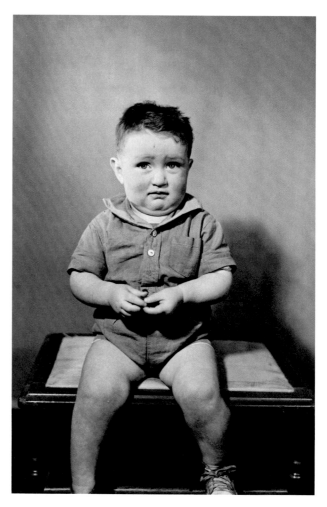

FIRST HAIRCUT ★ Francis J. Sullivan Studio ★ *Derry, New Hampshire, 1949*

8

Bachrach Studios ★ *East Coast, n.d.*

Delmar Watson Studio ★ *Hollywood, California, c. 1940's*

Francis J. Sullivan Studio ★ *Derry, New Hampshire, 1956*

George Durette Studio ⋆ *Manchester, New Hampshire, n.d.*

12

George Durette Studio ⋆ *Manchester, New Hampshire, 1931*

Harry Annas Studio ★ *Lockhart, Texas, n.d.*

Harry Annas Studio ★ *Lockhart, Texas, n.d.*

Paul Gittings Studio ★ *Houston, Texas, 1935*

John Deusing Studio ★ *West Allis, Wisconsin, 1929*

Joe Steinmetz Studio ★ *Tampa, Florida, 1958*

18

Jack Rodden Studio ★ *Roswell, New Mexico, n.d.*

Francis J. Sullivan Studio ⋆ *Derry, New Hampshire, 1959*

George Durette Studio ★ *Manchester, New Hampshire, 1939*

John Deusing Studio ★ *West Allis, Wisconsin, c. 1930's*

Orrion Barger Studio ★ *Chamberlain, South Dakota, 1957*

24

George Durette Studio ★ *Manchester, New Hampshire, 1940*   Delmar Watson Studio ★ *Hollywood, California, 1947*

Joe Steinmetz Studio ★ *Sarasota, Florida, 1963*

Samuel Cooper Studio ★ *Malden, Massachusetts, c. 1960's*

27

SECURITY NATIONAL BANK OPENING ★ Orrion Barger Studio ★ *Chamberlain, South Dakota, 1957*

HALLOWEEN PARTY ★ Orrion Barger Studio ★ *Chamberlain, South Dakota, 1952*

29

BETTY'S FIRST BIKE ★ Orrion Barger Studio ★ *Chamberlain, South Dakota, 1948*

★ THE SUBJECT

Betty's First Bike, 1948

What we see in a photograph and its meaning for us will change when we correct any false assumptions we might have about the subject it portrays. In this case a wrong assumption could be that Orrion Barger, the photographer, was hired by Betty's parents to photograph her on the occasion of her getting a bicycle for her birthday.

BETTY, *May 1978:*
It certainly was my first bike. It happened just before school started. I think it was the chamber of commerce that sponsored a kids' day. There were lots of games and there was a drawing for a bike. I won. Nothing like that had ever happened to me before in my life. They had two bikes but I picked the boy's. I was a tomboy. The bike was red and I think it was a Schwinn. It was the prettiest bike I'd ever seen in my whole life. The picture was taken for the newspaper.

If I hadn't won that bike I never would have owned a bike at all. My father didn't believe in bikes. He would have thought it was a waste of money — money was to pay your bills and buy food. But he rode the bike when I brought it home. I had my good dress on. In fact it was the only dress I owned. We wore dresses to school then and I wore it every day and washed it out every night. I wore blue jeans at home, but not the nice ones they have today.

Having the bike didn't change my life all that much. If I didn't get my work done I didn't get to use the bike. I shared it with my neighbors and with my sisters.

On a typical day in my house I got up and listened to my father tell me what he wanted me to do — my chores. He said things only once and my mother never stepped in. He was the boss and he expected all of us to work hard. That rides with you through life. My father also put in my mind that once you are married you are married.

Both my mother and father worked and they believed we should work too. We cleaned the house and got dinner and did the dishes. We also had livestock — cows, horses, and pigs — to take care of, and the raking and the mowing to do. It was during the Depression and no one had much money. We all worked hard unless we could get out of it, but I was always caught, so I could never get out of it.

I moved to Oacoma after I was married, because we were too cramped in Chamberlain. My husband was from a farm and we are now on a semi-farm. I also work in Al's Oasis and my husband is also an independent trucker. I'm still at it really — work I mean, and farming.

I have three of my own children, one niece, and a foster child living with me. I'd take in more if I had the room. TV, movies, and cars have softened life for kids today, but mine still have chores to do, but not as hard as my father's. I have tried to teach them that if you do your work well you can be proud of yourself. You can be as good as anybody. You have to go along with life. Some are born with silver spoons and some aren't. It doesn't matter if you are colored, Indian, rich, or poor. If you respect yourself others will respect you, and you get a lot of self-respect through work. My foster child is an Indian and my niece is an Indian. My own children are French, German, and Irish mixture. My husband is German.

I'd rather be in the Black Hills or Colorado than in Oacoma. It's too crowded here. The population is only about two hundred,

31

so that may sound funny to you, but there are too many people close around me and I don't like to feel pushed in. I've been trying to get to Colorado since I left Chamberlain and I have only gotten five miles.

I don't know why you want to use that picture. I don't take a good picture.

You know, the picture was taken when I was in the fifth grade, and we just threw away the frame of the bike about one-and-a-half years ago. My mother kept it and put it away after I was married, and my daughter and my oldest son rode it. The honor roll is now gone too from Main Street.

The photograph has not changed, but our new knowledge of Betty has very much altered our understanding of it. And Betty is only part of the subject of this picture. The photographer, unlike the painter, does not dispose of any of the objects and people captured by the framing. A small length of Main Street appears in detail, and one wants to know about the little girl in the long dress so beautifully surrounded by the frame of the bike, or how a wad of gum got on the tire of a brand-new bike won on kids' day, or how Barger's presence affected Betty's posing.

RAINBOW CAFE TEEN CANTEEN ★ Orrion Barger Studio ★ *Chamberlain, South Dakota, 1957*

Harry Annas Studio ★ *Lockhart, Texas, 1956*

Terry Wood Studio ★ *Tupelo, Mississippi, c. 1960*

34

Jack Rodden Studio ★ *Tahota, Texas, n.d.*

YOUNG MAN AT PIANO AND WITH DEER ★ O. B. Porter Studio ★ *Houlton, Maine, 1938*

Martin Schweig Studio ★ *St. Louis, Missouri, 1959*

★ TIME & PLACE

St. Louis, Missouri, 1959

The interpretation of a photograph depends upon knowledge of the culture at the time it was made.

THE PHOTOGRAPH ON THE FACING PAGE, taken in 1959, shows three self-satisfied, neatly dressed young Americans who are proclaiming themselves to be beats, which they clearly are not. Is this simply a waggish pose or is there more to it than that?

The year 1959 marked the end of the Eisenhower era. Public-opinion polls showed that Americans were smug about their country and their lives, and there was good reason for this: the United States was more prosperous than any nation in history. There was little sense of national guilt, such as would come in the succeeding years of civil-rights protest and Vietnam; Americans seemed unaware of the poverty and prejudice that existed in the midst of the affluence.

During the nineteen-fifties, America glorified its children. With Dr. Spock in hand, adults allowed their lives to be child-centered. Photographs of homes at Christmas look like pictures of disheveled toy stores. But while most of the adults were indulging themselves and their families, there was a movement among the urban young to withdraw from work, family, education, and the good life. These were the beats.

Signs of this movement included the popularity among first college and then high-school students of J. D. Salinger's book *The Catcher in the Rye*; the idolatry of James Dean, who starred in the movies *East of Eden* and *Rebel Without a Cause*; the cult that developed around Jack Kerouac; the identity crisis as a newly coined phenomenon to describe the painful transition from adolescence to adulthood; and the publication in 1960 of Paul Goodman's influential *Growing Up Absurd*, in which he decried the lack of a meaningful adult life in America. To the disaffected, adulthood seemed difficult and unfulfilling —not worth the effort.

What caused young people from affluent families to rebel, or at least to identify with those who did? Perhaps many of them had grown up in fatherless homes during World War II; the theme of the absent or ineffectual father runs through the literature and analytic studies of this time. It may be that young people looked around and, like the photographer Robert Frank, saw an America where the themes of family, work, and country had been replaced by empty and lonely faces, automobiles, and prejudice. The young had been told that America was a country of unlimited choices, but from what they saw they were beginning to question the value of all choice. Personal freedom in the affluent society seemed meaningless.

Some responded to the contradictions in our culture by becoming beats, some only by admiring alienated heroes such as Salinger's Holden Caulfield and Hollywood's James Dean; others at least showed awareness of the times—look at the people on the opposite page. In America commercialism often turns behavior into fads, and yet one should not discount the cultural genesis of the picture. Although the three young people in no way look like beats, they were responding, humorously and perhaps part seriously, to real pressures that were starting to be felt in America.

Harry Annas Studio ⋆ *Lockhart, Texas, 1930*

40

Hamblin Studio (W. E. A. Moore) ★ *Suffolk, Virginia, c. 1931*

HASTY PUDDING ON TOUR (all male Harvard University club) ★ Joe Steinmetz Studio ★ *East Coast, 1937*

Terry Wood Studio ★ *Tupelo, Mississippi, n.d.*

O. B. Porter Studio ★ *Houlton, Maine, n.d.*

Joe Steinmetz Studio ★ *Heinz Pier, Florida, 1941*

46

Hamblin Studio (W. E. A. Moore) ⋆ *Suffolk, Virginia, c. 1930's*

Joe Steinmetz Studio ⋆ *Sarasota, Florida, 1941*

BROOKLYN DODGERS
Joe Steinmetz Studio ⋆ *Vero Beach, Florida, 1949*

John Deusing Studio ★ *West Allis, Wisconsin, n.d.*

Joe Steinmetz Studio ★ *Sarasota, Florida, 1949*

C. Bennette Moore Studio ★ *New Orleans, Louisiana, c. 1939*

52

C. Bennette Moore Studio
New Orleans, Louisiana, n.d.

Joe Steinmetz Studio ★ *Florasota Gardens, Florida, 1952*

54

MARRIAGE MART ★ Joe Steinmetz Studio ★ *Elkton, Maryland, 1937*

Delmar Watson Studio
Hollywood, California, 1947

Francis J. Sullivan Studio ★ *Derry, New Hampshire, 1954*

Orrion Barger Studio
Chamberlain, South Dakota, 1938

Paul Gittings Studio ★ *Dallas, Texas, c. 1932*

Paul Gittings Studio ★ *Houston, Texas, 1930*

60

Paul Gittings Studio ★ *Houston, Texas, 1929*

George Durette Studio
Manchester, New Hampshire, 1938

Paul Gittings Studio ⋆ *Houston, Texas, c. 1930*

Paul Gittings Studio ★ *Houston, Texas, 1929*

Orrion Barger Studio ★ *Chamberlain, South Dakota, 1949*

Paul Gittings Studio ★ *Houston, Texas, 1929*

Harry Annas Studio
Lockhart, Texas, n.d.

Joe Steinmetz Studio ★ *Pennsylvania, 1940*   Francis J. Sullivan Studio ★ *Derry, New Hampshire, 1954*

Joe Steinmetz Studio ★ *Pensacola, Florida, 1958*

Joe Steinmetz Studio ⋆ *Longboat Key, Florida, 1958*

C. Bennette Moore Studio ⋆ *New Orleans, Louisiana, c. 1940*

Joe Steinmetz Studio ⋆ *Sarasota, Florida, 1959*

74

★ THE MAN WITH A CAMERA

Joe Steinmetz

The photographer selects the subject, the frame, the moment, the vantage point, the camera, and the lens when he makes a photograph. Photographs do not copy but transform reality.

THE PICTURE OF THE BURGER QUEEN on the facing page is a two-dimensional black-and-white illusion that looks better than the hamburger stand itself.

The picture pulls one in by the many lines of perspective whose vanishing points seem to converge at the base of the central canopy. This is unsettling because rather than receding to some distant spot, the canopy has a forward thrust that suggests it is about to take off from the paper on a fantasy flight.

Joe Steinmetz has taken a picture of a three-dimensional structure, yet the photograph flattens the space to bring everything forward to a single plane. At first the eye is drawn back to the road, farther back to the fence and the people, then to the hamburger stand itself, and finally to a drive-in theater. The next moment one notices the wispy overburdened palm tree that appears to be holding up the overlapping roofs, and the strange ferns that support the curb. The picture becomes a plane consisting of carefully distributed geometric shapes and spaces. The extraordinary sharpness of the near and the far, the tropical white of the buildings against the solid darkness of the cloud-pierced sky, the lack of informative shadows, and the use of both overlapping and separated shapes contribute to the mystery of the photograph.

Steinmetz's artistic urges may conflict with his realistic intentions, but it is clear that his first loyalty is to the subject. A root beer is ten cents and a cheeseburger thirty. Tickets can be purchased to the adjacent drive-in. Water looks like water and dried-out grass like dried-out grass. The hamburger stand is presented frontally with the honesty of a Victorian portrait.

The modernity of Steinmetz's vision makes us admire this vernacular photograph; it is possible that the origins of much contemporary art photography can be traced to such sources, usually ignored in photographic history. Clearly, studio photographers know that good form makes a subject more accessible.

Joe Steinmetz was born in 1905 and he has been a photographer for fifty-two years. When asked what he tells someone who wants to go into photography he responds: 'Always maintain a curiosity about people . . . about life. There's a photograph in practically everything you see, from the moment you wake up until you go to sleep. Experiment and you'll make it. But be sure you love it.'

Steinmetz has a studio in Sarasota, Florida, and is still taking pictures. He is a natural historian; recognizing the importance of context, he has created some of his most exciting pictures by stepping back from the primary subject and capturing the surrounding social landscape. Whether he is making a record of the adventures of a family of tourists or photographing Florida for the chamber of commerce, his negative envelopes are filled with detailed information.

Joe Steinmetz Studio ★ *Venice, Florida, 1953*

Delmar Watson Studio
Hollywood, California, n.d.

Joe Steinmetz Studio ★ *New York, New York, 1939*

Hamblin Studio (W. E. A. Moore) ★ *Suffolk, Virginia, c. 1931*

Joe Steinmetz Studio ★ *Middleton, Pennsylvania, 1942*

80

Joe Steinmetz Studio ★ *Sarasota, Florida, 1958*

Hamblin Studio (W. E. A. Moore) ★ *Suffolk, Virginia, c. 1933*

C. Bennette Moore Studio ★ *New Orleans, Louisiana, n.d.*

Francis J. Sullivan Studio ⋆ *Derry, New Hampshire, 1949*

84

Joe Steinmetz Studio ★ *Phoenixville, Pennsylvania. 1940*

Terry Wood Studio ★ *Tupelo, Mississippi, 1956*

86

O. B. Porter Studio ★ *Houlton, Maine, 1938*

Delmar Watson Studio ★ *Hollywood, California, 1947*

Francis J. Sullivan Studio
Rockingham, New Hampshire, 1948

90

Orrion Barger Studio ★ *Chamberlain, South Dakota, 1953*

Jack Rodden Studio ★ *Roswell, New Mexico, 1963*

Jack Rodden Studio ★ *Roswell, New Mexico, n.d.*

Joe Steinmetz Studio ⋆ *Miami, Florida, 1955*

George Durette Studio ★ *Manchester, New Hampshire, c. 1930's*

George Durette Studio ⋆ *Manchester, New Hampshire, 1931*

Jack Rodden Studio ★ *Roswell, New Mexico, n.d.*

98

Jack Rodden Studio ★ *Roswell, New Mexico, n.d.*

Joe Steinmetz Studio ★ *Bay Shore Gardens, Florida, 1959*

O. B. Porter Studio ★ *Houlton, Maine, 1949*

100

Delmar Watson Studio ★ *Hollywood, California, 1947*

ROSE PARADE ★ Delmar Watson Studio ★ *Pasadena, California, 1952*

102

Harry Annas Studio ★ *Lockhart, Texas, c. 1950's*

Joe Steinmetz Studio ★ *Manasota, Florida, 1956*

104

Joe Steinmetz Studio
Bradenton, Florida, 1951

105

George Durette Studio ★ *Manchester, New Hampshire, 1940*

106

George Durette Studio ⋆ *Manchester, New Hampshire, n.d.*

George Durette Studio
Manchester, New Hampshire, 1932

Jack Rodden Studio ★ *Roswell, New Mexico, n.d.*

Francis J. Sullivan Studio ★ *Derry, New Hampshire, 1948*

110

Francis J. Sullivan Studio ★ *Derry, New Hampshire, 1953*

George Durette Studio ⋆ *Manchester, New Hampshire, 1935*

112

★ THE VIEWER

Looking at *Morte,* 1935

Past experiences, accumulated knowledge, interests, and values strongly influence what
a person sees when he looks at a picture, how he interprets it, the memory it evokes
in him, and the kinds of questions he asks.

THE PICTURE ON THE FACING PAGE is crammed with bare
facts. It appears less ambiguous and mysterious than many
photographs. But listen to what four people say when they
see the photograph.

VIEWER 1:

*I see a person who has passed away. It looks like a Catholic funeral,
because of the medallion and the prayer cards on the table. I've been
to a lot of Catholic funerals.*

*It brings to mind my grandmother when she was laid out like
that. Granny passed away when I was twenty-two. I had an eerie
feeling then, as if she would get up and talk to me. I am amazed at
how good a job they do. They are just sleeping. They are so alive.
I'm not shocked or upset at seeing a dead body so alive, but I'm not
looking forward to being one myself.*

*I don't particularly like going to a funeral. I go out of respect
for the living. People I hadn't seen in years came to my grandmother's. It is good to see all my cousins and aunts and uncles. It
takes a funeral or a wedding to get us all together. Dying was a real
community thing—everybody dropped by. We would look at the
body and go down to the smoke room and chew the fat and catch up
with what had been happening to everybody and their kids.*

*I had mixed feelings seeing her dead. My main thought was
that she is at last at peace. She had a lot of suffering for a long time.
If I have to go I want to go fast.*

*When my father passed away I didn't get the picture of his
being dead at all when I was looking at the body. But then they
started to put him into the ground and then I knew I would never
see him again. His death was real.*

*My daughter works at Polaroid and she says pictures come
through today with people in caskets. So the picture taking is still
going on. She says there are a lot of them. She doesn't want to
touch them.*

It's life—it's just very short.

VIEWER 2:

*I bet this was taken with a large camera and printed from a large
negative. I wonder how large the negative actually was? It has no
grain at all, and look at the tones. I can just feel that old paper and
its dustiness and the smoothness and slipperiness of that shiny satin.
You couldn't do that with thirty-five millimeter. I guess nobody has
taken pictures of dead people for centuries though. I wonder if any
funerals are still like this. Bodies seem to go to med schools or are
cremated. Think of all the work and time that went into setting up a
scene like that. It looks like a party. People had the time then. I
guess they didn't do it for everybody, though. She must have been
famous.*

*You can certainly tell the picture wasn't taken in California.
It's an old town. Even the flag has only forty-eight stars.*

I don't know anybody who has ever died. If my parents died I

*wouldn't have the vaguest idea what to do about it. The only thing
I know is that people nowadays don't buy flowers. They send the
money to a charity. Who sent all these flowers—friends, relatives,
the American Legion?*

*I just might try to take pictures like this. No one is doing
anything like this.*

VIEWER 3:

*I see a woman in her casket in her home for all to observe. She is
involved with the American Legion, so she must be middle-class. Is
that a fake clock? There is a marvelous old gaslight converted to
electricity and an electrified candle. What is that elaborate object
in front of the coffin? Does it support the coffin? Is that a rail so
people can parade by? I don't know what the funny little writing
tray with the two cups means. I guess it is her mother in the picture.*

*The emotional content of death is pretty well removed. It is a
scene for going through a conventional response to death as contrasted
to finding a dead body on the street. That's what the undertaker does
for you. You come in and you know how to behave. It makes death
ordinary—something we can handle. The important thing when you
are putting on a public event is that it is all set up so you know
exactly what to do. You can avoid anxiety. Death doesn't come
into it because there are no symbols of death—no gauntness about
her, no harshness.*

VIEWER 4:

*I had no idea! I've never been to a funeral like this. This is Man-
chester. Yes, I see it is in French, so she is French-Canadian.*

*There is a contrast here between opulence and this seedy little
room with a gaslight fixture and naked bulbs. I wonder if it is her
home. I almost always admire ritual, but I don't understand this.*

*Why is it so expensive? Is the American Legion doing it for the
mother of a former Post commander?*

*It is American fantasy with a price tag. It reminds me of the
difference between the whole new business of toys for kids and old
toys. New toys are spin-offs from TV and it is all there so kids
don't have to invent any of the fantasies. They are all ready-made.
There is very little room for spontaneous reaction. This is like that.
Why isn't her family around saying good-bye?*

*As I ramble on I realize she is lost. Your eyes go to the clock
—not to her or the religious objects. It is hard to catch her attention.
You should be thinking about her and instead you are thinking
about the scene. She is probably a hard-working, nice lady if you
can get past the politics. I imagine she is D.A.R., but even if I could
see her dress I don't know her well enough to know if she picked
it out. I do know a lavish funeral like that meant she was much
admired.*

*I went to three funerals of ninety-year-old relatives last year
and while they all had rituals, they were all WASPS and it was
all very restrained—Episcopal—no open caskets, but the casket was
there and it was something substantial and I spent a lot of time
thinking about the bodies inside them and you knew they were dead.
More so than here.*

*But why take a picture? Is it a comfort to someone, or a record
like a wedding album, or is it to say 'see the show we put on—we
didn't skimp'? I guess I really don't mind the opulence. It is the
picture I mind.*

These four viewers are friends who happened to visit my house
on the same afternoon. They hardly represent a random sample,
for they all come from basically the same social environment,
yet each brings to the photograph his or her unique way of
reacting to its content.

EASTER SUNRISE ★ Delmar Watson Studio ★ *Forest Lawn, California, 1947*

George Durette Studio ⋆ *Manchester, New Hampshire, 1937*

Harry Annas Studio ⋆ *Lockhart, Texas, 1955*

Paul Gittings Studio ★ *Houston, Texas, 1929*

Harry Annas Studio ★ *Lockhart, Texas, c. 1935*

120

Harry Annas Studio ★ *Lockhart, Texas, c. 1935*